MINECRAFT ZOMBIE

BOOK 2

BULLIES AND BUDDIES

First published by Herobrine Publishing in 2015.

Creator: Zombie, Zack, author.
Title: Zombie goes to camp / Zack Zombie.

ISBN: 978-93-5471-286-9

Series: Zombie, Zack (Fictitious character). Diary of a minecraftzombie ; 2
Target Audience: For primary school age.
Subjects: Zombies--Juvenile fiction.
Camps--Juvenile fiction.
Diaries--Juvenile fiction.

Typeset in Agent 'C' and Potato Cut TT
Published by Scholastic India Pvt. Ltd.
under license from Herobrine Publishing

This edition : August 2022
Printed in India at Saurabh Printers pvt. Ltd.

DIARY OF A MINECRAFT ZOMBIE

BOOK 2

BULLIES AND BUDDIES

BY
Zack Zombie

Koala Books

MONDAY

Whew!

We barely made it out of there alive. That's the last time I'm ever going to Steve's house!

You'd think that if a guy invited you to his house, he would let the neighbors know you were coming. But nooooooo... Steve forgot to tell his neighbors that a Zombie, a Skeleton, a Slime and a Creeper were all coming over for dinner.

So you can imagine how happy the villagers were to see us.

It didn't help that Skelee brought his bow and arrow. Or that he wanted to show everybody how good he could shoot.

It also didn't help that Creepy started getting nervous and shaking all the time. We had to keep calming him down every few minutes... I mean, every few minutes all we heard was, "HISSSSSSS..." Then a few minutes later, "HISSSSSSSS...."

Just when we thought he calmed down, we heard, "HISSSSSSSS!"

I don't think I'm going to take Creepy anywhere anymore.

After all that, Slimey tripped and broke into a bunch of little **SLIME PIECES.** Villagers were running around like crazy because he and his pieces kept running up to them to say "Hi." I don't think Slimey is good at reading social cues. He can be a bit thick sometimes.

Then the torches came out!

The villagers started screaming and yelling at us, waving their torches around.

Now, from my last experience with fire, I didn't want to stick around **FOR THAT!** I didn't want to have to stay home and grow my skin back again! So I was the first one to run out of there.

They even unleashed their dogs and cats on us. The cats were kind of cute, but the dogs were really mean. Actually, I think one of the dogs got a piece of

Skelee while we were running. All I remember is that when we got out of there, Skelee seemed shorter than usual. Also, he started **BOBBING UP AND DOWN** when he walked.

Creepy said that he didn't like the cats. He said that he didn't like how they kept hissing at him all the time.

We finally got out of there and made it back home.

I would say we got back in one piece but... Slimey was missing some of his small pieces. The dogs got a few pieces of Skelee. And Creepy was missing his arms.

Wait a minute... Did Creepy ever have arms?

Anyway, I dropped a few of my **BODY PARTS** as well. Nothing major. Just a few toes, and maybe a finger or two.

Well, that's the last time I'll ever go to Steve's house. Maybe next time he can come to my place instead.

TUESDAY

Everybody was back at school today.

Slimey got himself back together. I think Skelee found his lost pieces because he seemed taller again. Also, he didn't bob up and down when he walked anymore. And, even though I couldn't find my body parts, I think having a few less fingers made me look cooler to all the kids at school.

But, poor Creepy was traumatized by the whole experience. He stayed home from school today because his mom wanted to keep an eye on him. I think they said something about "24 hour watch," and something about preparing a **"BLAST RADIUS."** But I didn't really understand what his parents were talking about.

Adults can be weird sometimes.

After school, I found Steve mining as usual. I think he was really sorry for what happened the other day. He wanted to make it up to me, so he gave me his favorite video game.

"It's really cool," Steve said. "I think you'll really like it."

"What's it about?" I said.

"It's about Plants and Zombies."

I was surprised that humans would be so **INTERESTED IN ZOMBIES,** but I didn't get the Plant part.

"Really? What's so special about Plants and Zombies?"

"**JUST PLAY IT.** You'll see," Steve said.

"Cool. I think I'm going to play it with the guys at my sleepover this Friday. Thanks, Steve!"

Man, the guys are going to think I'm the coolest Mob at school when they see this video game! All the kids are going to be crawling over each other trying to come to my sleepover.

I'm going to be the most popular kid in school! I thought....

WEDNESDAY

I decided to walk Sally to school today.

One thing about Sally is that she really likes to talk.

She told me about everything that happened to her over the weekend. She told me about her mom, her dad, her big brother and little sister, her cousins, her pet squid, the weather, her operation, when she got her tonsils put back in, her pimple, and how proud she was that I faced the **IRON GOLEM.** She even talked about how weird it is that I have a human friend named Steve.

She likes to talk about everything! But I don't mind. I'm just glad she's my ghoulfriend. That's what Skelee told me I was supposed to call her. But, I don't think he really knows what he's talking about. He's never had a girlfriend or a ghoulfriend. But I'm sure he wishes he had.

Skelee tried to talk to a girl at school once. She was a

screamleader named Lotta Bones. She was really popular. But he chickened out.

The kids at school teased him, and told him he didn't do it because he didn't have the guts.

Well, in the middle of Sally talking to me, I think I made her mad.

Maybe it was because I started picking my **NOSE CAVITY** while she was talking.

Or, maybe it was because I was flinging my boogers in to the air while she talked.

Or, maybe it was because I found a really big booger that was connected to a long string of snot.

Or, maybe it was because I took that really big **BOOGER** with snot attached to it, and I ate it.

But I think the reason she got really mad at me was because I didn't share any with her.

How was I supposed to know that I was supposed to share my lunch with my girlfriend? Or ghoulfriend...or whatever I'm supposed to call her?

THURSDAY

I started telling all the kids at school about the new video game I got from Steve. I had all the kids drooling more than usual, wanting to play it.

"Where did you get it?" they asked.

"I got it from my human friend, Steve," I said.

"Oh man, then it must be awesome!"

Just the thought of doing something against the rules, like

playing a human video game, got all the boys at school jumping at the chance to come to my sleepover on Friday. Just in time too.

BIG MOUTH JEFF was going to have his sleepover this Friday too, and he already had about ten kids coming to his. I just had Skelee, Slimey, and Creepy coming to mine. And we can't always count on Creepy.

But, now that I have this video game, like twenty kids said they were coming to my sleepover. A lot of those kids canceled on Jeff and jumped on my list. Even Jeff came over and asked to come to my sleepover.

"Alright, Jeff, you can come," I said. "But, I have to pull a lot of strings to get you in."

Ha! Who's the **KING OF THE PLAY YARD** now?

I can't wait till the kids play my new video game. With a name like Plants vs. Zombies, it's gotta be a hit!

Wow... So this is what being popular feels like. Sweet.

FRIDAY

Today is the day of my sleepover. I have like 25 kids coming over. Mom and Dad had to buy tons of extra cake for all of the guys.

I'm so excited. This is going to put me on the map as the most popular kid at school!

I can imagine what my yearbook picture is going to say when I graduate: "The most popular Zombie that ever lived." Or, "The Zombie everybody in school wants to be."

This is awesome!

I've got to figure out what to do with my **LITTLE BROTHER,** though. I know he's going to try to bother all of my friends and bite them on the ankle. I'm thinking of hiding his chicken so he won't bother us.

Or, maybe I can hide him in the basement, with the other body parts we keep down there...

I know what you're thinking, but we don't keep human remains in the basement. Those are just extra **ZOMBIE BODY PARTS** we keep in case we lose a leg or arm at school or on the playground or something.

We have a big supply of arms, legs, feet, butts, ears, elbows, and fingers down there. Mom likes to make sure we are fully stocked and prepared in case anything happens. Dad says if there was ever a Human Apocalypse that we could survive in the basement for a whole year.

Sweet.

But, the little minion has got to go. I just have to think of something that won't get me in trouble with Mom.

Anyway, I'm all set for my sleepover tonight.

Got the food... Check!

Got the comics... Check!

Got the coolest video game in the world... Check!

SATURDAY

Oh, man, it was terrible! All the kids were horrified.

Some kid fainted and fell on the cake. Another kid lost his head... and we still can't find it. One kid's guts came out. It's so bad that he looks more like a Skeleton than a Zombie. Even Big Mouth Jeff was huddled in a corner rocking back and forth, crying for his Mommy.

All the kids went screaming and running home.

Slimey got out of the house so fast that he fell and broke into a bunch of Slimey bits again. He even left some of his Slimey bits behind at my house. I'm just glad CREEPY couldn't make it. I think if he did, we would all be in the hospital right now.

That video game showed us things that our young eyes should have never seen.

We saw Zombies getting eaten by plants...

Zombies being blown to pieces...

And even Zombies getting run over by lawnmowers!

It was horrible! I'm going to have "DAYMARES" for weeks!

I think the thing that really grossed us out the most was the part about Zombies eating brains. Yuckkk!!! That was the grossest thing I ever saw. Even writing about it, I think I'm going to hurl.

So much for being the most popular kid at school. Actually, I think I'm now the most unpopular kid on the planet.

Maybe I'll go live with the **HUMANS...** They might take me in.

I just need to stay away from their plants.

SUNDAY

I went to go see Steve to return his video game to him.

"It was really cool, right?" he asked.

I don't think he could tell from my empty eye sockets what I really thought about his game.

"Did you get to the part where the Zombies are on the roof?" he asked. "That's a tough level for me," he said. "I always get my brains eaten..."

I hurled.

"Whoa! Are you OK?"

"I'm OK. But I don't think that game was really my taste..." I said. Then I hurled again.

"Wow—you're really **HURLING CHUNKS** today," Steve said. "Well, maybe you might like this game. It's one of the best."

He handed me a cool looking video game. It looked pretty good. Maybe I could redeem myself at school with this one.

"Thanks, Steve," I said. Then I said **GOODBYE** and walked home.

I wonder what this video game is about. All I know that with a name like, "Call of Duty: Black Ops—Zombie Edition," it must be good...

MONDAY

"Mommy, Mommy! I have lice in my hair!"

That's all I heard when I woke up today. When I got out of bed, the whole house was going crazy! I asked my Mom what was going on. My Mom was jumping up and down.

"Your little brother got an infestation of lice in his hair!" she said.

"Whoa!" I said

"Let me check your hair!" she said.

I let my Mom check my hair. She went through it like she was doing brain surgery on me.

"Nope. **NO LICE,"** she said.

"Aw, Man! Why couldn't I wake up with lice in my hair?" Why is it that my little brother is always the lucky one?

My Mom and Dad were so happy for my little brother getting lice that they brought a cake home for him after school.

LIFE IS SO UNFAIR...

Most of the kids at school have lice. But for some reason I can't get any. I even thought if I slept on my little brother's pillow, I might get some. All I got when I woke up was boogers and chewing gum stuck to my face.

Man, some kids just have all the luck.

TUESDAY

Today we had Mob Gym class at school. That's when they get all of the mobs together in the gym to play games. They do it because they think we need the exercise. They don't want us to be like the chubby human kids that are suddenly popping up all over the place.

They decided to play a game called Dodge Ball. I thought it sounded like fun...until they started picking teams. Of course, Me, Skelee,

Slimey, and Creepy were the last to get picked. I heard that none of the other kids wanted us on their team. I think they were still mad at me about the sleepover.

The gym teacher decided to make us **OUR OWN TEAM.** I thought it would be fun playing with my best friends... Until...

All of a sudden the gym doors burst open and we saw "HIM" for the first time. When "HE" walked into the gym, all of the kids nearly fell apart. One kid dropped his jaw and it broke into a few pieces. The gym teacher turned so white he almost looked human.

"HE" must've been seven feet tall, and had a chest the size of a house. They said his name was **MUTANT,** and he had just transferred to our school.

I knew he was trouble as soon as I saw **MIKE MAGMA,** the bully, give him a high five. We're all doomed...

All I can say is that the game of Dodge Ball was really short. Mike Magma and Mutant were the only ones on their team because Mutant counted as 3 people. And of course, Mike Magma and Mutant's team demolished every team they played.

Now, because there was a rule that every kid had to play, we were the last team to face Mike and Mutant. Before we got up to play, we had to bench Creepy because he started HISSSING again. So Me, Skelee, and Slimey (who by the way is Mike Magma's cousin), had to play against Mike and Mutant.

Now, I thought the Iron Golem was scary...

And I thought Mike Magma was scary...

But, **MUTANT** terrified me.

They say Mutant got his name because his parents lived next

to a witch's hut in the Swamp Biome. I heard the witch cursed their family. She put a hex on them that would cause them to give birth to a Mutant baby Zombie. They were so happy.

I actually think they planned the whole thing. That would explain why they moved so close to the **WITCH'S HUT.**

Anyway, when "Mutant" was born, they say he was as big as a Zombie horse. Then he started growing and will probably never stop. Some kids even say that if he's hungry enough, he can eat an entire human village! And this is the guy we were up against!

Mike Magma

Mike Magma already had it out for his cousin Slimey. So I knew we were **DOOMED** for sure.

Mike threw the first ball really hard at Slimey and broke him into a bunch of Slimey bits. Then Mutant took the ball, which looked like a pea in his hands, and flicked it at Skelee. I don't think Skelee knew what hit him.

Next thing I know, I hear Skelee calling me from above. His head somehow ended up stuck to the gym ceiling. And who knows where the rest of his body went.

So, I was the last one left.

"YOU CAN DO IT!" Skelee yelled from the ceiling.

Mike Magma picked up the ball to throw it at me, which gave me some relief. But then he passed it to Mutant.

Mutant picked up the Dodge Ball with his fingers and flicked it at me. All I could do was pick up some of Slimey's bits to protect myself, and close my eyes...

Next thing I know, I heard everybody in the gym yelling and cheering. I opened my eyes, and Mike Magma and Mutant were lying on the ground **OUT COLD.** Creepy and Slimey's bits came over to congratulate me.

"What happened?" I asked.

"The ball bounced off of Slimey's bits you were holding and hit

Mutant so hard that it knocked him over. He landed on Mike Magma, knocking him out of the safe zone, and automatically disqualifying them. You won!"

Everybody picked me up and carried me out of the gym, cheering my name.

I closed my eyes so I could take it all in... **IT WAS AWESOME.**

Then I woke up. In the hospital.

WEDNESDAY

I stayed home from school today to recover from my wounds.

"Why do they play games like Dodge Ball in schools, anyway?" Mom asked. "It's so dangerous!"

"I think it toughens kids up," Dad said.

I didn't tell them about Mutant. Mostly because my jaw was in a glass jar next to my bed. But it's not like I didn't try.

"What was the name of the boy who did this?" Dad asked.

"MFRMNT!" I said.

"Mumford? How **TOUGH** can he be with a name like that?" Dad said.

"MUFRND!" I said.

"Buford? That's even sillier!" Dad said.

"MOOTRNRT!" I said really loud.

"Q Bert?"

"You kids and your games. Just be a little more careful next time.

Remember, it's all fun and games until somebody loses a body part."

Urrrrggggghhhh! Forget it. Parents just don't understand!

Creepy came over and told me that half of the kids from gym class are at home recovering too.

"The good news is that you missed the scare test that was scheduled for today," Creepy said. "You're lucky. It was really hard. We had to **SCARE** baby villagers. And they really creep me out."

I guess something good did come out of my suffering.

THURSDAY

One thing I love about being a Zombie is that we heal really fast. I guess it's because our body parts aren't really attached that well. It can be a little annoying though.

When I was a baby Zombie, I would always leave my butt on the potty. Then when I would go out to play, I couldn't understand why I always felt a draft.

Dad fixed it with some pliers, a little wire, a screw driver, and a really long screw.

The kids in gym class still ask me, to this day, why I have a screw for a **BELLY BUTTON.** I just tell them I was born that way. They usually

don't bother me after that.

Now today at school, Ms. Bones

told us that we had to make up the test we missed. I was so bummed. But, she did say we can skip it if we do extra credit homework. Hey, I like scaring baby villagers as much as the next Zombie, but extra credit is always easier.

My extra credit assignment was to bang on some village doors, and then pick up some vegetables from a villagers' garden to prove I did it.

PIECE OF CAKE!

After class, I went to a village close by. All the villagers ran into their homes when they saw me. This is going to be an **EASY A.**

I banged on some doors, which was fun. Then, the last thing I needed to do was to pick some vegetables.

I'll get some carrots, I thought. They're really easy to carry. So I grabbed a bunch of carrots, and started happily heading back home.

All of a sudden, I saw these small, beady red eyes looking

at me from the bushes. And no matter which direction I moved, they kept following me.

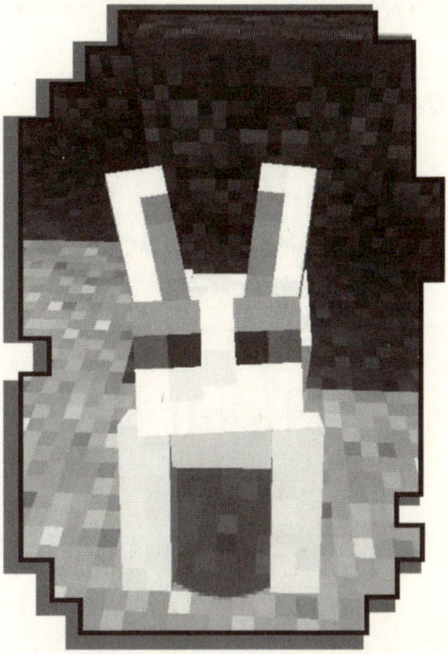

So, I got a little closer.

The "cute" little bunny rabbit

Next thing I knew, a cute, **LITTLE RABBIT** came out of the bushes. He was white and fluffy, but he had really red eyes.

"You hungry, little fella?" I asked him. "Have a little bite of my carrot."

All of a sudden, that cute, little rabbit tore my arm off, and made off with all of my carrots!!!

"KILLER RABBIT! KILLER RABBIT!!!" I yelled.

I was running around in a circle, yelling, and waving my remaining arm up in the air.

"KILLER RABBIT! KILLER RABBIT!!!"

Then I remembered that Killer Rabbits are only dangerous to humans, not Zombies.

So after I calmed down, I walked to where the rabbit was eating my carrots, and tried to reach over and grab my arm. It **GROWLED** at me. So I quickly grabbed my arm and ran back to school.

So much for my easy A.

FRIDAY

Today, I had to explain to Ms. Bones why I didn't have my extra credit homework.

"A Killer Rabbit ate my homework!" I said.

All the kids in class burst out laughing. I could tell that Ms. Bones was not buying it, either.

"I'm sorry, but I'm going to have to give you a failing grade," she said.

"No, a Killer Rabbit really did eat my homework!" I said. "I can prove it. See!" I showed her my **DISMEMBERED** arm.

She still didn't buy it. I think it's because I used the missing limb excuse a few times before.

"Sorry. Here's your F. Please have your parents sign your exam and bring it back on Monday."

On my way home, I thought, oh, man, when my Mom and Dad see this, I'll be grounded for a month.

Even worse, this is the weekend my Dad was going to raise my allowance. What am I going to do?

I had to think of something or I was probably going to be **GROUNDED** for life, not to mention be broke for the rest of my middle school life.

SATURDAY

I went to go see Steve to see if he could help me get out of the trouble I was in. When I found him, Steve was busy mining for diamonds.

"Hey, Steve!"

"AAAHHHH!!" Steve screamed. "Oh, man. You scared me. Why do you always sneak up on me like that?"

"Habit, I guess. Find any diamonds?" I asked.

"Nothing yet. But I know they're here somewhere."

"You know, Steve, you really shouldn't be mining at night. There's some really **SCARY MOBS** out at night."

Then I told him about Mutant.

Mutant can be a real pain . . . literally!

Steve's eyes got bigger and bigger as I told him my Dodge Ball story.

"Sounds like a bully to me," Steve said. "We've got them too. Just not as...gulp...big as Mutant."

"Well, I need your help with something," I said.

"I got an F on my extra credit homework and if I show it to my parents, I'll get in **TROUBLE** for sure. And this was the weekend my Dad was going to raise my allowance."

"Why did you get an F?" Steve asked.

"A Killer Rabbit ate my homework."

Steve looked at me for a minute, then he burst out laughing.

"Was that your excuse?" Steve said.

"No. It really happened. A little, cute, white rabbit with red eyes attacked me and ate my homework!"

Steve could not stop **LAUGHING.**

Then I thought about it for a

minute, and I burst out laughing too.

After five minutes of laughing, Steve said, "Well, if it really happened, just tell them the truth."

"If Ms. Bones didn't believe me, and you didn't believe me, my parents won't either."

"Parents will **SURPRISE** you sometimes. Just tell them the truth and see what happens," Steve said.

"Well, OK. But I'm not holding my breath."

"I thought Zombies don't breathe?" Steve said.

"**FORGET IT.**"

Then I walked home thinking about how my parents were going to react when I tell them that, "A Killer Rabbit ate my homework."

SUNDAY

Today I have to share the bad news with my parents. They're never going to believe that a Killer Rabbit ate my homework.

Maybe I could tell them that a human ate my homework? Naw. They know Steve is my friend, so I know that won't work. Or, maybe I could tell them that my little brother ate my homework? Naw, he has an alibi... He was with my Mom all day.

I guess I'm going to have to tell them the truth.

I still don't understand why nobody believes me. I mean, are Killer Rabbits that rare?

If they are, maybe I can catch it and sell it to the **MOB ZOO** or something.

At least that way I won't be totally broke, since I'm probably not going to get any allowance till I'm thirty.

Well, here it goes...

SPECIAL SUNDAY ENTRY

I can't believe it... My parents actually believed me.

Best of all, I got the raise in my allowance!

It was kind of strange, though, that when I mentioned the Killer Rabbit, they looked at each other like they knew something... I wonder if they know where the Killer Rabbit came from.

I mean, my Dad does work at a **NUCLEAR WASTE PLANT.** And my Mom also works there as a secretary. I remember one time they told me that there were a lot of rabbits that lived around the Nuclear Waste plant.

They even tried to bring one home once... But my little brother was creeped out that the rabbit had three eyes.

But anyway, who cares. What matters is that I got a raise in my allowance! And now I can buy myself my own video games.

No more borrowing games from Steve. His games always get me in trouble.

The last game he lent me got me sent to the **PRINCIPAL'S OFFICE.**

They even called my parents in to tell them about my, "Inappropriate recreational choices," whatever that means.

But who cares. I'm just counting my Benjamins.

MONDAY

Today I was feeling so good.

My parents weren't mad at me for failing my extra credit homework. The kids at school have almost forgotten about the sleepover incident. And I got more money in my pocket.

It looked like it was going to be a good day. Until...

On my way to school, I got stopped by Mike Magma and

Mutant. Oh man! I knew I was going to either end up in a dumpster, or get a **ZOMBIE WEDGIE** that I would feel for weeks. But it looked like these guys wanted to torment me a little more than that.

"Pick him up," Mike said.

Next thing I know, I'm hanging upside down, because Mutant picked me up with his fingers.

"Shake him," Mike said.

Mutant began to shake me up and down like a salt shaker. All of my money started falling out of my pockets.

"Shake him some more," Mike said.

Then I started dropping fingers, a few teeth, some ribs and a leg bone or two. Mike picked up all of my money.

"Drop him," Mike said.

Next thing I know I was **IN A HEAP** on the ground with all my body parts. I think Mutant picked up one of my ribs to pick his teeth with. Then they walked away laughing.

I pulled myself together as best as I could and made it to school. I didn't want the kids to know that those bullies **TOOK MY LUNCH MONEY.**

"There goes my allowance," I mumbled to myself.

Man... Being a Zombie in Middle School is hard.

TUESDAY

I had my Mom drop me off at school today, so I could avoid running into Mike and Mutant. I know I was setting myself up for potential embarrassment, but it's better than getting eaten by Mutant.

I thought about telling my Mom about what happened yesterday, but I know she would freak out and make a scene at school. Not only will I be embarrassed at school, but Mike and Mutant would probably get me for telling on them. So I decided to talk about my "**FRIEND**" instead.

"Mom, I have a friend at school that is getting bullied. And, I feel really, really, really bad for him. What should I tell him to do about it?"

"Well, son. You should tell one of the teachers right away. They can talk to the bully's parents and then the bully's parents will have a nice talk with their bully child. And then everything will be OK," Mom said.

I could only imagine telling Ms. Bones about Mike and Mutant.

Then I could imagine Ms. Bones calling Mike and Mutant's parent's in. Then I could imagine Mike and Mutant's parents having a good talk with Mike and Mutant. Then I could imagine Mutant **EATING** me and my whole family, just for telling on him!

"Mom, what if the bullies get mad if I tell on them...Errr... If my friend tells on them?"

"Well, the teachers can talk to their parents again," Mom said.

Of course, by then, Mutant would be picking his teeth with my leg bone, and wearing **MY SKULL** as an earring. I didn't have the heart to tell my Mom that her advice would lead to my early death, so I just stayed quiet.

I asked Mom to drop me off next to the school yard behind the school. I got out of the car and thought I was safe from getting embarrassed by my Mom in front of the kids at school.

I only made it ten feet, when my Mom yelled out loud, "Honey, bunny! Doesn't your Mommy get a kiss goodbye?"

All the kids heard it and started laughing. Then I had to do the walk of shame back to my Mom to give her a kiss in front of all the kids.

"**SMMMAAACCCkkk.**" My Mom gives really long kisses. Then she gave me a hug that felt like it was ten minutes long. All the kids were snickering.

Mom's hug felt good, though. I think she knew that it was me who was getting bullied, and she wanted me to know she **UNDERSTOOD.**

It was still really embarrassing, though.

WEDNESDAY

I thought about what Mom said yesterday, so I decided to talk to Ms. Bones about my bully problem. After class, I stayed behind to talk to her.

"Can I help you with something?" she asked.

"Um...Ms. Bones. I...Errr...have a problem..."

"Spit it out, young man. Don't stand there and mumble," she said.

Ms. Bones was not the nicest teacher in the school. She was **REALLY STIFF.**

"Errr... I have a friend that is getting bullied. And I wanted to ask you what he should do..."

"Tell that young man to talk to me this instant! I'll have a meeting with these bullies and their parents. And if we have to, we will suspend them from school!"

All I could think about was Mike and Mutant dedicating their entire lives to getting revenge on me for getting them suspended from school.

"Uh... **MS. BONES...** It's not a big deal. I just heard about it from another friend, who heard it from his friend, who heard it about a Zombie in another school. I'll be sure to tell them what you said."

So I chickened out. It was a good thing I did too. On my way home, I ran into Mike and Mutant again.

Mike said, "I saw you stay after class and talk to Ms. Bones. You weren't talking about me and Mutant, were you?"

"Because, if you were, things would get extremely **PAINFUL** for you..." Mike said, smiling.

All Mutant would do is stand there and grunt. "Urrrrggghhhh."

"I didn't say anything. I swear! I was just looking for more extra credit homework to do..."

"Well, you better not. Otherwise my friend Mutant over here will use your legs as chopsticks, and your arms as toothpicks. Got it?!!!"

"Yeah... I got it. He, he... I'll be going now..." I said.

As I walked away, I could see Mike and Mutant **STARING** at me all the way home.

Boy, am I in trouble.

Later that night, I thought about asking my Dad what he would do. Dads are cool like that.

And my Dad looked like the kind of person bullies would pick on at school.

I went into Dad's office and I

asked him, "**HEY DAD,** how do you handle bullies?"

"Why, son? Is someone bullying you at school?" Dad asked.

"No, no. I have a friend that has a friend that knows this boy in another school that...Err...thinks he's being bullied."

"Well, son, I had my share of bullying when I was a kid. Come to think of it, it used to happen a lot actually."

"How did it stop?" I asked him.

"Oh, my Dad got a new job in another Biome, so we moved to another school."

GREAT. *Now I have to join a witness protection program and get relocated,* I thought.

"But if you want to handle bullies, the best thing to do is to stand up to them and show them you're **NOT AFRAID.** When they realize you are not easy to push around, they usually leave you alone."

I just imagined standing up to Mike Magma and Mutant. I

imagined telling them, "You are not going to bully me anymore!"

Then I imagined Mutant stepping on me and using my remains as a rag to wipe his big forehead.

"Does that help son?" Dad asked.

"Sure, Dad. Thanks," I said, as I walked away thinking about my life as a sweat rag.

THURSDAY

To take my mind off of my bully problem, I thought about Slimey's birthday party coming up this weekend.

I really love birthday parties at Slimey's house. His parents go all out. But best of all, they're going to have lots of cake!

My favorite part of the party is always the Piñata. They always make it into cool shapes. This

The Ghast Piñata

year they made it into the shape of a Ghast.

We get to stuff tissue in our eye sockets and then whack the **PIÑATA** with a stick.

One time, we stuffed one of the fat Zombie kids full of candy, and then whacked him with a stick. It was the funniest thing ever.

The Zombie fat kid was laughing, too, so I guess it didn't hurt. As I was getting ready this morning, though, I was shocked. My face was full of the biggest pimples you ever saw!

But the part that shocked me most was that one of my pimples was shrinking! Oh man, all of the kids at school are going to see and they're going to tease me.

"You look like you got a patch of **HUMAN SKIN** on your face," They're going to say.

Or, "Whoa, look at the size of that pimple! It's so small. Man, I would hate to be you."

I bet Sally is going to see it, and she's going to treat me like I got "Hooties." (Hooties are human cooties by the way.)

I rummaged through the medicine cabinet to see if I had any pimple **GROWING CREAM.** All I saw was Mom's make-up kit. Maybe I can add some make-up to my face to make it look like my pimple is bigger. I put on everything I could find. But the pimple was still small!

I got an idea, and I got some glue and a marble. I glued the marble on top of the small pimple, and added make-up on top of it.

Yeah, that'll do it, I thought.

I just have to keep my head really still until the glue dries. So, no sudden moves and I'll be OK.

"**HEY HONEY.** Wants some breakfast?" my Mom yelled.

"Sure, what are we having?" I said as I came downstairs.

"Zombie eggs and Mooshroom stew."

"Again? Man, just for once I would like to have cake for breakfast."

"What's that on your face?" Mom asked.

"Uh... I was scratching my pimples a lot yesterday to see if I could get them to grow. And one of them grew really big."

"Don't scratch them too much or you might pop them. Remember, you want them to be nice and ripe, and **FULL OF PUS,"** Mom said. "You want to look your best for the party this weekend, don't you?"

"Sure. OK. Mom."

I tried to keep my head still as I walked to school. I was trying to balance myself with my books in one hand and my lunch bag in my other hand.

I was doing **PRETTY GOOD** when all of a sudden; I felt something next to my leg. I wanted to look down, but I couldn't move my head or the marble would pop out.

Something crawled up my pants leg and into my shirt. I tried to move around a little bit, but the marble on my face started coming off.

Oh, Man... What is that?

It felt **SMALL AND FLUFFY.** And it was fast. I tried grabbing it with my hand in front, but it moved to my back.

All of a sudden, I saw some white, long fluffy ears in front of my face. Then I saw two beady red eyes looking at me.

"IT'S THE KILLER RABBIT!!!"

"KILLER RABBIT!!! KILLER RABBIT!!"

I started running around in circles, waving my arms, and screaming. The Killer Rabbit grabbed my lunch then took off into the bushes. I picked up my books and ran to school. I got there late, so I ran straight into class.

Next thing I know all of the kids and Ms. Bones are staring at me.

Then one of the kids yelled out: "CRATER FACE!!!"

Then all of the kids start laughing. Even Ms. Bones started

laughing. I ran out of class and straight to the bathroom.

I looked in the mirror and I saw a **VOLCANO** on my face! I had put so much glue on that when the marble came out, it looked like I had a lunar crater on my face.

I tried to scrape off the glue, but it was too hard. Worst of all, I had to go back to class, and look like this all day.

It was the most terrible, horrible, no good, worst day...Ever!

FRIDAY

I woke up this morning and I ran to the mirror.

I was doomed. My pimple was gone. All that was left was a big space where my pimple used to be. I guess this means I'm not going to Slimey's party tomorrow.

I walked down to breakfast, and my Mom and Dad's first words were: "Whoa! Son, you're missing a giant pimple from your face."

As if I didn't know already.

Then my little brother started poking me in the space where my pimple used to be.

"STOP IT!" I said.

"Mumma, Dadda—Zombie's got a hole in his face..."

"Urrrrgggghhhh!!! Can't everybody just see that my life is over!" I yelled.

"Don't worry, Honey. We've all had it happen to us," Mom said.

"Maybe you can use some of your Mom's make-up to cover it up," Dad said. "You know, when I was a kid, we used to glue marbles on our face and cover it with makeup." Dad laughed. "The hardest part was waiting for the glue to dry..."

Oh boy.

"Don't worry, honey, it'll grow back," Mom said.

"How long is it going to take, Mom?" I said.

"Oh...about a week."

Oh boy...

I tried to use every trick in the book to keep from going to school. But my parents weren't buying it. So off I went to school with a big hole on my face.

When I got to school, I was already getting looks from everybody.

One guy looked at me like I had **TWO HEADS.** Which was funny because he had two heads...

I guess I've got to get used to being treated like some weirdo, and all because my skin is clearing up.

I wonder if Steve ever goes to through this.

Probably not.

Anyway, before I got to class, my **GHOULFRIEND,** Sally, stopped me. She had a big bandage on her face. I asked her if she got another operation. But she told me that her face started clearing up too. She thinks she got it from her cousin who came to visit her. And she thinks she gave it to me.

"How long does it last?" I asked Sally.

"Just two days," she said. Then she handed me a bandage to put on my face.

"Just tell everybody we were in a **BIKE ACCIDENT,"** she said.

Sally is the best ghoulfriend a Zombie could have.

So all through school, kids were asking me what happened.

"I was in a motorbike accident," I said. "Yeah, me and Sally were doing about 100 miles an hour, when all of a sudden the bike got away from me. We were lucky to survive. Just a few scratches on our face."

Worked like a charm. Kids thought I was the coolest thing since **SLICED MOLDY BREAD.** Having a ghoulfriend really does improve your street credit. Especially in middle school.

SATURDAY

I woke up this morning and guess what? My pimple came right back bigger, fatter and filled with juicy pus and everything! I was so happy.

Now I can hold my head up high. Not to mention I can go to Slimey's party without having to wear a bandage on my face.

I made it to Slimey's party and all the kids were already there. I looked for Slimey, and he was taking pictures with Skelee.

"WASSUP?" I said.

"Wassup?" Slimey said back. Then we burst out laughing.

"Hey, is Creepy coming today?" I said.

"Yeah, he should be here in a little while. I think his Mom took him to buy a suit for the party.

"Where'd they go?" I asked

"I think they went to the Bomb Supply store to get one," Slimey said.

"Cool. Any cake left?"

"Yeah, we got a whole lot. My Mom and Dad really went all out," Slimey said.

Well, everything at the party was going great. Until...

Mike Magma, Slimey's cousin, showed up with Mutant.

OH BROTHER. Here we go again.

I guess they couldn't tell him to leave because he was a part of Slimey's family. But this time,

Mike brought a gift for Slimey.

Slimey was touched and actually thought Mike had changed his ways. But when Slimey opened the box, there was a **KIDDIE POOL** inside.

"Go ahead, blow it up," Mike said, with Mutant standing beside him.

Slimey blew up the kiddie pool, knowing what Mike was going to do next. Mike got a hose and filled the kiddie pool with water. Oh man, this was going to be bad.

"Now get in," Mike said to Slimey.

I felt so bad for Slimey, especially because Slimey can't swim... Even in a kiddie pool.

Slimey got in the pool and started thrashing around, and calling out for his Mommy and Daddy.

We all felt **SO BAD** for him, but what could we do? Mutant was standing right next to Mike, and if we tried to say something, he would've eaten all of us, and then had cake for dessert.

Slimey's Mom and Dad ran out and saved him from the kiddie pool. By then, Mike and Mutant took their piece of cake and left the party. Kinda ruined it for everybody.

Man, I've got to do something about those guys.

One of these days they're going to get what's coming to them...

SUNDAY

I decided to go see Steve today to ask him about my bully problem.

Steve wasn't mining when I found him. He had a brewing stand, and he was mixing a bunch of potions together.

All of a sudden, Kabbooooomm! The brewing stand blew up in his face.

"Are you alright, Steve?" I asked him.

"Cough, cough, cough! Yeah, I'm

good. That's the fifth time today. Sixth time is the charm."

"What are you trying to do, anyway?" I asked him.

"I'm trying to turn cobble stone into diamonds. It sure would make mining so much easier," he said.

"Hey, Steve, I have a question to ask you..."

"SHOOT."

"Shoot what?" I said.

"No, I mean sure. Go ahead and ask," Steve said.

"Well, have you ever had anybody bully you?"

"Oh man, a while ago, I was bullied by one of the meanest, ugliest, and dangerous bullies you have ever seen," Steve told me.

"Who was he?" I asked, thinking this might help me out!

"His name was Harry O'Brian. But most of the kids just called him **HEROBRINE,** for short. This guy was so mean that he would hurt anyone who looked at him funny."

"He used to like to play with fire too, so he used to burn everything up."

"So what did you do about him?" I said.

"I decided to stand up to him."

"Really?" I said.

"I was scared, because I knew he could hurt me," Steve said. "But I couldn't stand being bullied anymore. So I told him in a strong voice to 'STOP!' And then he stopped, and I never saw him again," Steve said.

"Whoa..." I said.

See, that's why I like talking to Steve. He's so tough. I just need to be more like Steve.

You know, I think that is what I'm going to do. I'm going to look like Steve and act like Steve, and this way I am going to be as tough as Steve. I'm going to stand up to those bullies once and for all!

When I got home, I was thinking about the first thing I would do to be more like Steve. I was thinking about **PUNCHING A TREE,** but I was already missing a few fingers, and I didn't want to lose anymore.

Or maybe I could collect rocks. But, I'm still not sure what Steve does with them.

I know what I'll do. I'm going to cut my hair to look just like Steve.

I got my Dad's hair clippers, and I started cutting my hair into a block shape. It was kind of hard since I didn't have that much hair on one side of my head. But I was determined.

When I finished, it looked a bit **LOPSIDED.** But I think it was still cool.

Afterward, I went down to dinner, and as soon as everyone saw me, they dropped whatever they were holding.

Then I heard my little brother say,

"Mummy, Daddy... It's Gumby!"

I guess my hair was a bit more lopsided than I thought.

"Son, what in the world did you do to your hair?" Mom asked.

"I wanted to try a new hair style. This is called the **BLOCKHEAD,"** I said.

"The Blockhead? Is that the new style the kids are wearing nowadays?" Dad asked.

I didn't have the courage to tell them I was trying to look like Steve, my human friend.

"Yeah, Dad. It's really popular," I said.

"Are you sure?" Mom asked. "Because it looks a little... Well... Human."

"**TRUST ME,** Mom," I said. "I'm one of the coolest kids in school."

They both looked at me with a confused look on their face.

"Gumby, Gumby, Gumby..." was all I heard throughout the rest of dinner.

Little brothers are so annoying.

MONDAY

I woke up this morning with morning hair. So instead of waking up lopsided, my head looked like an arrow. I didn't have time to fix it because I was late.

As I ran out the door, I think I heard my parents laughing in the house.

I couldn't wait to face Mike and Mutant at school today. I was going to give them a piece of my mind.

Just so happened, that Mike and Mutant ran into me on the way to school. As soon as Mike saw me, he burst out laughing.

"Did you get your head caught in a pencil sharpener?" he sneered. Mutant just stood there staring.

"I got an idea," Mike said. "Looks like you forgot to put gel on your hair this morning. I think we can help you with that. **RIGHT, MUTANT?"**

All of a sudden, I heard Mutant make the loudest hacking noise I have ever heard.

Oh man, I knew what was coming next...

Then he spit into his hand. But you couldn't see it because his hands were so big. Next thing, he balled up the **SPIT WAD** in his hand and flicked it at my head.

Next thing I know, half of my body is covered in Mutant's snot.

"That should help you manage that craaazzzzyyy morning hair!" Mike said. Then he walked away laughing.

Mutant wiped his hand on the

other side of my body and then walked away with Mike. So there I was, covered from head to toe with Mutant's snot.

OLD MAN JENKINS was strolling by with his Zombie horse when he saw me.

"What in tarnation are you up to this time?" he said.

"I got slimed..." I said. Then I burst out crying.

"There, there, young man... It happens to the best of us," he said. "But I've got the perfect remedy for that."

Next thing I know, his **ZOMBIE HORSE** started licking all of the snot off of my body, face and head.

"There you go. Good as new," he said. "Though I don't think there's anything we can do about your hair..."

I told Old Man Jenkins the whole story about the bullies. He nodded his head like he understood everything I was going through

"You know," he said. "One of the best ways to stop a bully is by helping them."

"What do you mean?"

"Well, what I've found is that most kids become bullies because somebody bigger was bullying them. Help them with their bullying problem, and you'll probably make a **FRIEND FOR LIFE.**"

Make friends with Mike and Mutant? No way! And if somebody bigger than Mutant was bullying him, what was a little guy like me supposed to do about it, anyway?

I didn't want to disagree with Old Man Jenkins, especially since his horse just licked snot off of my face.

"Thanks, Mr. Jenkins," was all I could say.

As he strolled away he said, "You're welcome, son. Just remember, bullies are just scared little kids, who are being bullied themselves!"

Somebody is bullying Mutant? That's really **HARD TO BELIEVE.**

TUESDAY

At school today they decided to show a movie about bullying to all the kids. I think Ms. Bones spoke to the Principal about the conversation I had with her.

The movie was in black and white and it was really old. It was about a little skeleton that was being bullied by a creeper.

The creeper would threaten to beat up the little skeleton unless he gave the creeper his lunch money. The little skeleton told his teacher, and he told his parents. The teacher called the creeper's parents and they had a talk with the creeper. The creeper apologized to the little skeleton, and the little skeleton was never bullied again...

Then, after school the creeper got his **REVENGE**, by beating up the little skeleton. But the little skeleton had enough of being bullied, and brought his bow and arrow to school the next day.

The next time the creeper tried to bully him, the little skeleton shot him with his bow and arrow. The creeper blew up and dropped a music disc.

Now the little skeleton listens to the music disc every day to remind him of his great victory! Yeah! I know. That's not how the movie ended. I made up that last part.

But telling my parents, really? Or telling the teacher, really? I know it takes guts, but Mutant is going to rip out my guts and use them as floss for his three teeth.

What's really interesting is that after the Bullying movie, all the kids were given wrist bands that said, "Stop Bullying!"

And all the kids that wore them got bullied even more.

WEDNESDAY

Today we had a field to trip to the Zombie farm where they had Zombie horses.

All the kids got a chance to ride one. I never rode a Zombie horse before. But, I got a really nice green one.

A Zombie Horse

Skelee got a Zombie skeleton horse that looked really cool.

Slimey had a hard time staying on top of his horse. I don't know why; it wasn't that hard.

Creepy started getting really nervous around the horses, so the teacher called his Mom to come take him home.

The Zombie horse trainer gave us instructions on how to ride the Zombie horse.

He said, "Zombie horses are **SPECIAL.** They do the opposite of a regular horse."

"When you want your horse to start moving, just say 'Stop!'"

"When you want your horse to stop, just say '**GIDDYUP!**'"

"When you want your horse to move really fast, just say 'Whoa!'"

"And if you want your horse to jump, just say 'Yeah!'"

He made us all repeat everything three times so that we wouldn't forget. Skelee wasn't paying attention because he was busy playing with his Zombie horse.

Skelee's Dad takes him to regular

horseback riding all the time, so I think he thought he knew what he was doing. So when we all started moving, he fell behind because he didn't know how to get his Zombie horse moving.

I went back and told Skelee to say 'Stop!' to get his horse moving.

"'**STOP!**' That doesn't make any sense!" Skelee said.

So Skelee said 'Stop!' and his horse started moving.

When we caught up with

everyone, Skelee said "Whoa!" to get his horse to stop. All of a sudden, Skelee's Zombie horse took off running really fast.

He kept saying, 'Whoa! Whoa! Whoa!' And his Zombie horse kept running faster and faster.

Skelee's horse was about to reach a cliff, when the Instructor caught up to him and yelled, "Say Giddyup! To get him to stop!"

So right when Skelee was about to reach the cliff, he yelled, "Giddyup!".

The Zombie horse stopped dead in its tracks, right before it went over the cliff.

We were all happy Skelee was OK. I could see Skelee from far away, and I gave him a **THUMBS UP.** He gave me a thumbs up back and yelled, "Yeah!!!"

THURSDAY

Skelee stayed home from school today to recover from going over that cliff. It's a good thing Skeletons heal fast too.

After school today, I decided to go visit my Mom and Dad at their job at the Nuclear Waste plant. I wanted to see all of the rabbits that Mom said lived around there.

At the plant, Dad showed me all of the machines they use to

collect Nuclear Waste. It was kind of boring, but it made my Dad happy.

"Dad, what do they do with all of the **NUCLEAR WASTE?"**

"Oh, we pump it into the water supply that we drink everyday... That's what gives us the nice shade of green in our skin," he said.

"Cool."

Later, Dad had to do some work, so I decided to go see if I could find some rabbits. I saw a cute brown one, but it ran away. I chased it into the bushes.

While I was going through the bushes, I saw a house on the other side. It looked more like a shack than a house, but I could tell someone lived there.

The little brown rabbit ran out of the bushes into the field next to the shack. I was going to go after it, but next thing I know, **MUTANT** came out of the house!

Oh, man that poor rabbit is dead,

I thought. Mutant's probably going to eat him in one bite.

Next thing I know, Mutant sat next to the bunny rabbit and the rabbit jumped into his lap. I couldn't believe it. Mutant was stroking the little rabbit with his finger.

Then a bunch more rabbits came out and jumped on Mutant's lap and on his head and his shoulders. I could not believe my **EYE SOCKETS.**

Suddenly, a midget Zombie came out and started yelling at Mutant.

"What are you doing, you big Ogre!" he yelled. "Are you playing with those rabbits again? How many times do I have to tell you that rabbits are for eating, not playing with?!!!"

"You are the **DUMBEST** little brother anybody could ever have... I wish you were never even born!"

I don't know what came over me, but that last thing he said just made me so mad.

I jumped out of the bushes and yelled, "Leave him alone!!!"

"Stop saying those mean things to him. Can't you see that you're hurting his feelings?!!"

The midget Zombie said, "You want to stand up for this **BIG, DUMB, LOSER?** Why don't you take him home with you! We don't want him."

That was it. I picked up the little midget with my hands and I said to him, "My Mom and Dad work at the Nuclear Waste plant next door. If I come by here again, and I ever hear you say something mean to Mutant ever again, you're going to be sorry!"

Well, I think I scared that little midget Zombie real good because he turned as white as snow. As soon as I put him down, he went **RUNNING** into the house.

Then Mutant stood up...

Well, I thought he was going to step on me for sure. But then, a cute, white, fluffy rabbit came out of the bushes and jumped on Mutant's shoulder.

Oh man, it was the Killer Rabbit from before! But this time, the little rabbit was gently rubbing against Mutant's face. Then he hopped over to me, and jumped on my head.

Mutant looked at me...and

SMILED.

We got home later, and I was still weirded-out from what happened today.

All I know is that Old Man Jenkins was right when he said that bullies are just scared little kids that are being bullied themselves.

Now, I don't know if Mutant will stop bullying me. But, at least I know his midget older brother is going to think twice before he bullies Mutant again.

It really does **FEEL GOOD** to stand up to a bully, especially when they're bullying the bully that bullies you.

FRIDAY

Today I didn't see Mutant in school. I was afraid that Mutant's older brother did something to him. I saw Mike Magma, though. But he wasn't acting as tough as he usually does when Mutant is around.

Good thing too. We had an all school Mob Gym class today again. And for some reason the gym teacher thought that we should play another game of Dodge Ball.

Like my Dad, the gym teacher thought it would toughen us up.

I actually think the gym teacher found out that Mutant was not in school today, and that's why he wanted to try Dodge ball again.

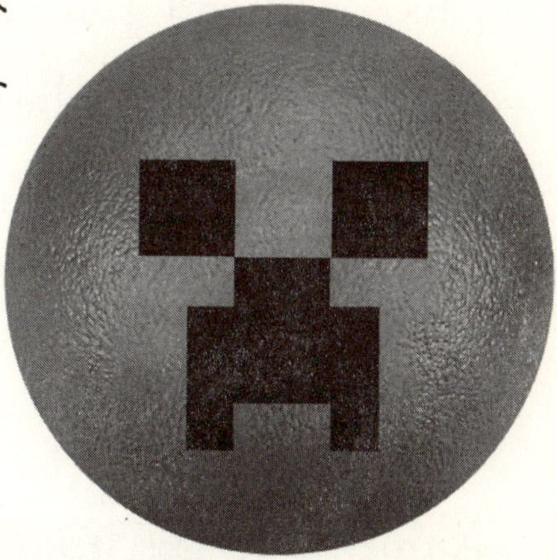

We had to play dodgeball . . . again!

Me, Skelee, Slimey and Creepy were picked last...again. So we made our own team **AGAIN.** We called ourselves "The Running Dead."

Kinda funny, since Zombies can't run. We just hobble really fast.

Mike Magma found the toughest, meanest, and ugliest kids he could find to be on his team. Somehow he found all of the bullies in school to join him.

Again, the **DODGE BALL** game was really short, because Mike Magma's team crushed every other team. And, because every kid had to play, we were the last team to play against Mike's team. We didn't stand a chance because we had to bench Creepy again. So it was just three of us against Mike and his goons.

We won the coin toss, so we got a chance to throw the ball first.

Skelee wanted the first throw to get Mike back for getting his head stuck in the ceiling. Skelee threw the ball as hard as he could at Mike. Since Mike was a **MAGMA CUBE** he just bounced up into the air and the ball missed him.

One of Mike's goons picked up the ball really fast and threw it at Slimey. Unfortunately Slimey couldn't jump as high as Mike, so Slimey burst into a bunch of Slimey bits when the ball hit him. I think Mike was mad because he wanted to be the one to smash Slimey into little bits.

Now there were only two of us.

But, Skelee was **AMAZING!** He did a leap into the air while throwing the ball at one of Mike's goons. The goon didn't even see it coming. It knocked his Zombie head right off. His body was just running around waving his hands in the air, not knowing which direction to go. They had to stop the game and get him and his head off the court. I could hear the crowd cheering. But then Mike hurled the ball with all of his might at me while they were getting Headless off the court.

All of a sudden, Skelee jumped in front of the ball to protect me from getting **SMASHED.** The ball hit Skelee right in his ribs and cracked a few. Skelee had to sit out for the rest of the game because he was hurt and in too much pain.

Now there was only little me against big Mike Magma and his two goons. I just imagined myself dreaming in the hospital again. Until...

All of a sudden the gym doors burst open. In came Mutant, shaking the ground with his feet as he walked across the gym.

Everyone in the gym went quiet. The gym teacher turned white, again.

Mike got really happy and went over to Mutant to give him a **HIGH FIVE.** I knew I was going to die. But then, Mutant walked right by him, like he didn't even see him.

He walked over to my side of the court, and I thought he was going to step on me or something. Instead he turned to me and gave me his finger for a high five.

Everybody in the gym was **SPEECHLESS.**

Then Mutant turned and faced Mike and his goons. The gym teacher blew the whistle, and we had the ball. Mike's goons on the other side were frozen solid with fear, and turned as white as a sheet. So, I made my move and threw the ball at one of them.

"You're out!" The gym teacher yelled.

Man, I got one! We could actually win this.

Mike was really mad by now. He got the ball and he tried to throw it as hard as he could at me. But he couldn't get a clean shot because I hid behind Mutant. He threw, and **MISSED!**

Then we got the ball. Mutant picked up the ball and looked at the other one of Mike's goons. That guy got so freaked out by Mutant that he hobbled really fast out of the gym. In fact, he hobbled so fast that he dropped a few body parts along the way. I think I saw him drop his spine somewhere next to the bleachers. Classic!

Then Mutant looked at Mike. Mike looked a little scared, but then he started yelling at Mutant.

"What's the matter you dumb, **OGRE?!!!"** he screamed. "Don't you know how to throw a ball?!!!"

"You're just a BIG....DUMB... LOSER! And I wish you were never born!!!" Mike said.

Then, all of a sudden something happened to Mutant. I could see him get really sad. And then I saw a tear come out of one of his eye sockets. He just stood there, frozen. I now figured out that Mutant had more than one bully in his life.

Mike kept taunting Mutant with meaner words.

Then, I just **SNAPPED...**

I took the ball from Mutant's hands, closed my eyes and threw the ball with all my might at Mike Magma. Next thing I know, I hear the loudest roar come out of the gym. I opened my eyes and all I saw were tiny Mike Magma bits all over the gym floor.

WE WON!

All of the kids picked me up and start cheering my name. I pinched myself to make sure I wasn't dreaming in a hospital bed somewhere.

I looked back, and Mutant is still standing there. The kids put me down and I went over to Mutant. I looked at his giant eye sockets. And I give him a smile.

Mutant looked at me, and he smiled back.

Then he picked me up and put me on his shoulders and we walked out the door. Then the kids give out a loud cheer. And then Mutant gave out a loud cheer. Then the whole gym came **CRASHING DOWN...**

SATURDAY

Yesterday was the best day ever.

We won the big Dodge Ball game at school. Mike Magma is no longer bullying me or any other kids at school. And best of all, I have a new friend named Mutant.

Mutant is actually a really nice Zombie.

The problem he had was that when kids saw him, they got

really scared of him. And he just felt lonely because no one ever wanted to play with him.

What really made me think was that he told me that he had been bullied for a long time, but he felt afraid of telling anybody. He would only talk to his rabbit friends because he knew they would listen.

I was the first person to ever stand up for him, and he really appreciated that. Plus, his Killer Rabbit didn't eat me, so he thought, I must be cool. I know...

I thought Killer Rabbits only bothered humans.

FIND OUT WHAT HAPPENS NEXT!

IT'S SCARE SCHOOL HOLIDAYS – and **Zombie's** going on a SCAREcation to **Creepy World!** But he's got Zombie puberty, his annoying little brother **AND** a

ZOMBIE KARATE TEST

to deal with first!